TOUCHDOWN!

THE HISTORY OF FOOTBALL

VIC KOVACS

CRABTREE
Publishing Company

FOOTBALL SOURCE

Author: Vic Kovacs

Editors: Marcia Abramson, Petrice Custance

Photo research: Melissa McClellan

Design: T.J. Choleva

Cover design: Samara Parent

Proofreader: Janine Deschenes

Editorial director: Kathy Middleton

Prepress technician: Samara Parent

Print coordinator: Margaret Amy Salter

Consultant: R Ian Smith. President. Ontario Football Alliance

Production coordinated by BlueApple*Works* Inc.

Cover images: 1892 Yale University Football Team; Kenny Washington, in 1946, the first African American player integrated into an NFL team; 1933 football card of Jim Thorpe, first president of the NFL

Title page image: Fullback Paul Byrne, Georgetown

Photographs

Cover: Public Domain (top left, middle left); Associated Press: © AP Photo (right); Shutterstock.com: © Dan Thornberg (bottom left); © Brocreative (bottom right)
Interior: Alamy Stock Photo: © Lee Foster (p 12 right); Critical Past: p 30 top; Shutterstock.com: © wavebreakmedia (TOC); pbombaert (page numbers); © Steve Broer (TOC background); © Aspen Photo (p 10 left); © Joseph Sohm (p 24); © Noel Moore (p 26–27 bottom); Keystone Press: © Kyle Okita (p 17); © John Pyle (p 18 bottom); © Michael Prengler (p 19); © Michael Prengler (p 21 bottom right); © Imago (p 26); © Sergei Bachlakov (p 29 bottom); Library of Congress Prints and Photographs: Harris & Ewing (title page, p 7 middle, 20–21 bottom, 23); Thure DeThulstrup (p 6 bottom); F. J. Higgins (p 6 middle); Corner Bookstore (Ithaca, N.Y.) (p 8 left); National Photo Company Collection (p 9 bottom, 20–21 top); George Grantham Bain Collection (p 10 right); Warren K. Leffler (p 12–13 top); Bain News Service (p 12–13 bottom, 12 left, 18 top); C.M. Bell (p 13 right); E.C. Kropp Co. (p 16 left); Public Domain: p 4; 5 top; p 5 bottom; Goldin auctions (p 6–7 top, p 7 bottom, p 12 top); p 7 top; p 8 right; p 9 top; Pach Brothers(p 9 bottom middle); p 11 left; p 11 right; p 13 bottom left; University of Pittsburgh Historic Photographs (p 14); p 15 top; p 15 right; p 16 right; p 20 top left; p 20 left bottom; p 20 bottom right; p 21 top right; p 22; Courtesy of the Gerald R. Ford Presidential Museum (p 7 bottom, p 13 bottom right); Creative Commons: Anthony Quintano (p 26–27 top, 27 left); nflravens (p 27 top); p 27 bottom right; tewarianuj (p 28 left); John Griffiths (p 28 right); Alain Falieres (p 29 top); p 29; AleXXw (p 30 bottom) Photofest: p 25

Library and Archives Canada Cataloguing in Publication

Kovacs, Vic, author
    Touchdown! : the history of football / Vic Kovacs.

(Football source)
Includes index.
Issued in print and electronic formats.
ISBN 978-0-7787-2297-7 (bound).--ISBN 978-0-7787-2302-8 (paperback).--ISBN 978-1-4271-1731-1 (html)

    1. Football--History--Juvenile literature. I. Title.

GV950.K68 2016   j796.33209   C2015-907472-X
                                          C2015-907473-8

Library of Congress Cataloging-in-Publication Data

Names: Kovacs, Vic.
Title: Touchdown! : The history of football / Vic Kovacs.
Description: New York : Crabtree Publishing Company, [2016] | Series: Football Source | Includes index. | Description based on print version record and CIP data provided by publisher; resource not viewed.
Identifiers: LCCN 2015045111 (print) | LCCN 2015042516 (ebook) | ISBN 9781427117311 (electronic HTML) | ISBN 9780778722977 (reinforced library binding : alk. paper) | ISBN 9780778723028 (paperback : alk. paper)
Subjects: LCSH: Football--History--Juvenile literature.
Classification: LCC GV950.7 (print) | LCC GV950.7 .K68 2016 (ebook)
LC record available at http://lccn.loc.gov/2015045111

Crabtree Publishing Company
www.crabtreebooks.com   1-800-387-7650

Printed in Canada/012016/BF20151123

Published in Canada
Crabtree Publishing
616 Welland Ave.
St. Catharines, ON
L2M 5V6

Published in the United States
Crabtree Publishing
PMB 59051
350 Fifth Avenue, 59th Floor
New York, New York 10118

Published in the United Kingdom
Crabtree Publishing
Maritime House
Basin Road North, Hove
BN41 1WR

Published in Australia
Crabtree Publishing
3 Charles Street
Coburg North
VIC 3058

CONTENTS

FROM ENGLAND TO AMERICA!   4

COLLEGE FAVORITE   6

FATHER OF AMERICAN FOOTBALL   8

COLLEGE FOOTBALL GROWS   10

SAFETY CONCERNS   12

THE BIRTH OF THE NCAA   14

COLLEGE BOWLS   16

CHAMPIONSHIP GAMES   18

GOING PRO   20

THE BIRTH OF THE NFL   22

NFL TODAY   24

SUPER BOWL GAMES   26

FOOTBALL IN CANADA   28

FOOTBALL AROUND THE WORLD   30

LEARNING MORE   31

GLOSSARY AND INDEX   32

WIN THE DAY!

FROM ENGLAND TO AMERICA!

Football, as it's played today, is a truly American game. Its origins, however, are more British than you might think.

Tough Game

Football-type games go back at least as far as ancient Greece and Rome. These games are the ancestors of soccer and rugby, which **evolved** into football. Historians believe that the games spread with the Roman empire, especially in Britain. By the eleventh century, British boys were playing a tackling game using an inflated cow bladder as a ball. These games were so rough that players could be seriously injured or even killed. By the 1600s, a soccer-like game had developed. Players could only touch the ball with their feet. The big change that led to football came in 1823, at Rugby School in England, when a player named William Webb Ellis grabbed the ball and ran with it. Within a few years, running with the ball became an official part of rugby.

When Rugby School students went on to universities, they took the game with them.

4

Humble Beginnings

The first games played in the United States were much closer to soccer and rugby. As the game evolved, different teams played by different rules, causing widespread confusion.

This 1865 artwork shows Civil War soldiers playing football in camp.

This led to a series of conferences that attempted to make a consistent set of rules for everyone. As play became more similar between teams, the sport became more and more popular. Today, football is the most watched sport live and on television in the United States. It has been reported as the country's most popular sport since 1985.

Gridiron Playing Field

The full name of America's most popular game is actually gridiron football. This helps to separate it from soccer, which other parts of the world usually refer to as football. This **unique** name came from the appearance of the original football fields, which had lines that ran the length and width of the field.

The grid pattern can be seen clearly in this 1910 postcard of the Syracuse University stadium.

This made it look like a checkerboard, or a kind of grill used for cooking called a gridiron. Even after the game got rid of the length lines, the name stuck. Today, it can refer to both the sport itself or the field it's played on.

5

The first recorded game of North American football took place on November 6, 1869. The contest was between two universities: Rutgers and Princeton. The rules used for the game were based on those used by the London Football Association, with a few changes. After this historic game, the sport began to catch on with other colleges, especially those in the northeast. Certain schools within a group of **elite** schools known as the Ivy League were **early adopters**, such as Yale and Columbia.

Rutgers has a proud football history. They beat Princeton 6-4 in the very first college game.

Rival schools Yale and Princeton had the top teams in early college football.

Picking the Style

Schools tended to play by their own unique versions of soccer rules, with one big exception. Harvard University played a sport called the "Boston Game," which was more of a cross between soccer and rugby. In May 1874, they played a series of games against McGill University from Montreal. The first game used Harvard's rules, while the second used McGill's, which **incorporated** more features from rugby. The American team found they enjoyed this style of play so much they quickly adopted it, and began spreading it to other schools.

When Harvard played McGill in 1874, a round ball was still being used.

Footballs grew more oval in shape after the forward pass was added to the game in 1906. The oval ball is easier to grip and flies better through the air.

The Ball

The first balls used for football were round, much like soccer balls. As more rugby influences came into the sport, and especially after the Harvard-McGill games, the ball began to take on more of an oval shape. This made it easier to carry and toss. The materials that went into making the ball were also upgraded. The first balls were actually pig bladders filled with air. This is why they're still sometimes referred to as pigskins. Today, the balls are made of plastic or rubber, covered with cowhide leather, and laced up with vinyl.

COLLEGE FOOTBALL GROWS

Football first emerged on college campuses, and it is no surprise that the game is still extremely popular at institutions of higher learning. Today, attendance at games often reaches into the tens of thousands, while TV broadcasts can reach millions. The current record for attendance at a single game was achieved in 2013 when 115,109 people attended a game between Michigan and Notre Dame at Michigan Stadium. Even in its early days, the game quickly became something of a **phenomenon**. By 1905, college football games often attracted more spectators than professional baseball games, which was impressive considering football's amateur status.

Crowds just keep getting bigger for college football in the U.S.

10

Spreading Out

By this time, the sport had also spread throughout the country. It extended first to schools in the Midwest, such as the University of Michigan and the University of Chicago, and then eventually south and west. As more teams emerged, so did various conferences or divisions, which grouped teams from neighboring areas together for play between colleges.

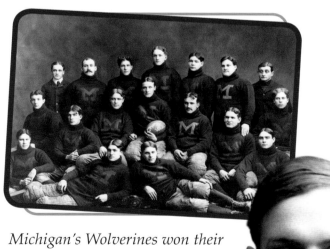

Michigan's Wolverines won their first conference title in 1898.

The 1902 Rose Bowl

The first postseason game played in college football history took place on January 1, 1902. The championship now known as the Rose Bowl was first called the Tournament East-West football game. It brought the University of Michigan's Wolverines all the way to Pasadena, California to play against Stanford, the best college team on the West Coast. At least 8,000 people showed up to watch the game, which ended with a score of 49 to 0, an overwhelming victory for Michigan. It was also the first bowl game played on New Year's Day, which has since become an annual tradition.

Neil Snow, a fullback for Michigan, set a record that still stands by scoring five touchdowns in the first Rose Bowl game. He was named Most Valuable Player of the game.

11

SAFETY CONCERNS

Early football was a dangerous game—so dangerous, that sometimes it turned deadly. In its early days, the game was played much differently. The forward pass had not yet caught on, so **mass-momentum** plays were often used to move the ball forward. The most famous of these plays was called the flying wedge. In these plays, the **offensive** team would form into a V-formation and charge the defense. They used their momentum, and other brutal means, to plow through or over them. Even after the flying wedge was banned, this style of play often led to horrific injuries like broken backs, bruised skulls, and broken ribs.

Since proper protective gear was in its early stages, using a rough style of play was a very effective strategy.

The NCAA Hall of Champions in Indianapolis, Indiana, displays this life-size bronze statue depicting the flying wedge as a salute to the early days of college football.

Saving Lives

In 1905 alone there were 18 player deaths and 159 serious injuries nationwide. The epidemic of injury and death became so bad that the president at the time, Theodore Roosevelt, was forced to **intervene**. He held a meeting with representatives from Harvard, Yale, and Princeton, who all left promising to take measures to make the game safer.

President Roosevelt began his safety campaign with Harvard, Yale, and Princeton because they were the top football schools at the time. A Princeton-Yale game is shown above.

*Leather helmets kept evolving for a few decades, adding more padding and switching from soft to hard leather. Wearing helmets was still completely **voluntary** until 1943.*

The Evolution of the Football Helmet

Originally, football was played without safety equipment of any kind. This began to change by 1893, when Joseph Reeves wore a padded cap made of leather in the Army-Navy game. In 1896, player George Barclay came up with a design that incorporated straps that would allow the helmet to close tightly around his head and protect his ears. Leather helmets ruled the game until helmets made of plastic appeared in the mid 1940s. These eventually became standard equipment. Today, helmets are expertly engineered, with professional models even incorporating technology like radio receivers, enabling players to hear calls and plays.

THE BIRTH OF THE NCAA

Unfortunately, Roosevelt's meeting did not lead to much change. This lack of action led Henry MacCracken, Head of New York University, to organize a meeting of 13 schools. Amid cries from various groups to ban football outright, this meeting led to a decision to attempt to reform the sport to make it safer. Afterward, invitations to all football-playing institutions were sent out.

On December 28, 1905, 62 schools came together to create a committee to standardize safer rules for the sport. The committee officially established itself as the Intercollegiate Athletic Association of the United States (IAAUS) on March 31, 1906.

New York University's Henry MacCracken launched a campaign to make college football safer after a player from his school was killed.

Modern Rules

The most significant rule change to come out of the IAAUS's first meeting was the legalization of the forward pass. This made football the game we recognize today. Other changes included shortening the length of games, and allowing teams to gain 10 yards instead of five for a first down. In 1910, during the group's fifth annual meeting, the name was changed to the National Collegiate Athletic Association, or NCAA—the name we know today.

One of the first jobs of the new athletic association was to put together a football guide, which was published in 1907. With official rules in place, the game became safer.

The Air Attack

Although a few teams had experimented with it previously, the first legal forward pass happened on September 5, 1906, during a game between St. Louis University and Carroll College. St. Louis quarterback Bradbury Robinson had tried it once unsuccessfully, but on his second attempt, the ball was caught by his teammate Jack Schneider. Eddie Cochems, the St. Louis coach, was so enthusiastic about the new play that he is often called the "father of the forward pass." Today, it's almost impossible to imagine the game without it.

Bradbury Robinson, who became a doctor, believed passing would help to make the game safer.

15

COLLEGE BOWLS

As the rules became more definite and the game became safer, football's popularity continued to soar across the country. The first Tournament East-West football game had been disappointing because of its one-sided win, and wasn't brought back until 1916. When it was, it proved to be such a popular part of Pasadena's Rose Parade festivities that in a few short years it had a stadium built specially for it. This stadium, called the Rose Bowl, is where the tournament got its name. By the 1930s, other warm-weather cities realized what a tourism booster these events could be, and started up their own bowl games. The most famous of these are the Orange Bowl in Miami, the Sugar Bowl in New Orleans, the Sun Bowl in El Paso, and the Cotton Bowl in Dallas.

This 1941 postcard shows the words "Sugar Bowl" spelled out on the field at Tulane Stadium.

The Orange Bowl trophy really is a bowl full of oranges. The football game and parade in Miami help to encourage people to visit sunny Florida.

Playing the Bowl

Colleges are grouped into different divisions by the NCAA based on factors like size, budget, number of athletic scholarships, and level of training facilities available.

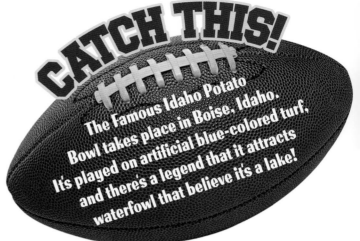

CATCH THIS!

The Famous Idaho Potato Bowl takes place in Boise, Idaho. It's played on artificial blue-colored turf, and there's a legend that it attracts waterfowl that believe it's a lake!

The top division, Division I, includes the best-of-the-best college teams. Bowl games are used as **postseason** games. Teams are awarded bowl spots based on their performance during the regular season as well as by their membership in different conferences.

Over the years, dozens of smaller bowls have come and gone, attempting to bring some money and fame to their town. Today, there are over 40 bowls that schools take part in, many with unique features!

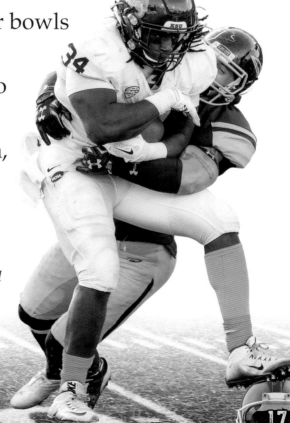

College teams may wear special colors to help a good cause. This player's team wore pink to promote the fight against breast cancer. A new bowl that started in 2015, the AutoNation Cure Bowl, also aids breast cancer awareness and research. It will take place every December in Orlando.

17

CHAMPIONSHIP GAMES

Though bowl games could be considered college football's championships, the NCAA has never held an official championship series. As a result, there have been different attempts by other groups to determine a national champion. The longest running

Princeton has one of the longest-running college football programs. The team has won 14 national championships.

of these is a poll taken by the Associated Press. This poll, taken since 1936, is voted on by sportswriters from all over America. Their choice is generally recognized as the champion. However, there have also been attempts to create championship tournaments.

The last team to win the BCS National Championship was Florida State, which defeated Auburn at the Rose Bowl in January 2014.

College Football Playoff National Championship

From 1998 to 2013, the Bowl Championship Series (BCS) took up this challenge. Using a combination of poll results and computer-determined standings, the top NCAA teams were invited to the top bowl games. The top two teams selected would play in the BCS National Championship Game, which rotated from participating bowl to bowl annually. In 2014, this complicated system was replaced by the College Football Playoff. In this new system, a committee votes on the top four teams from the NCAA's top division. These teams are paired off for two semifinal games, with the winners facing off in the College Football Playoff National Championship. Though not sponsored by the NCAA, the winner is generally considered the national champion.

The first team to win the new College Football Playoff National Championship was Ohio State, shown celebrating after defeating Oregon in January 2015.

GOING PRO

When football first started, there were no professional players or athletes who were paid to play. In fact, there were rules against paying athletes. Some athletic clubs got around these rules by obtaining jobs for their players, or by giving them expensive gifts that they could sell for cash. In 1892, William "Pudge" Heffelfinger became the first person to play the game for cash when he received $500 to play for the Allegheny Athletic Association against the Pittsburgh Athletic Club. Another one of the first players to accept money to play was John Brallier, who was paid $10 plus expenses to play a game for the Latrobe Athletic Association in Pennsylvania in 1895.

John Brallier, a quarterback, and Pudge Heffelfinger, a guard (inset), were top players of their era.

Latrobe was also the first team to play a season with a team made up entirely of paid professional players, in 1897.

Joining the Club

In 1899, an independent pro team calling themselves the Morgan Athletic Club started up in Chicago. After a series of name changes, they eventually became the Chicago Cardinals, and after a few moves, they ended up in Phoenix. Today they're known as the Arizona Cardinals, making them the oldest pro team still playing in the NFL. Other independent pro teams followed, with Ohio having as many as seven teams at once!

In 1920, the Cardinals joined the early NFL.

In 2015, Jennifer Welter became the first woman to coach in the NFL as an intern, or trainee, with Arizona. She coached and played for the Texas Revolution before that.

CATCH THIS!

Just two years after finishing their careers, many NFL players have money problems.

The First Scandal

When money is involved, things can get messy quickly. The sport's first major scandal happened in Ohio in 1905. The Canton Bulldogs coach and a Massillon Tigers player were accused of trying to fix games by getting one team to lose on purpose. Then, anyone who was part of the scam could bet money on the other team to win. Although nothing was ever proven, fans felt betrayed and abandoned the two teams, leading to them being shut down.

THE BIRTH OF THE NFL

As more independent teams emerged, small regional leagues began to form around them. With its large number of teams, one of the biggest of these local leagues was the Ohio League. By 1920, these early leagues were facing a few problems, such as growing player salaries and top athletes hopping from team to team for better offers. Teams were also recruiting college players before they had even graduated. Hoping a strong national league, similar to baseball's, would solve these issues, representatives from five teams met at a Hupmobile auto dealership on August 20, 1920, in Canton, Ohio. This meeting resulted in many of the Ohio League teams forming the American Professional Football Conference. Within a month, teams from Illinois, New York, and Indiana had been recruited, and the name was changed to the American Professional Football Association (APFA). Jim Thorpe was voted the association's first president.

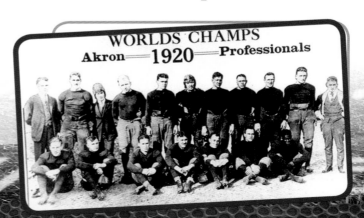

WORLDS CHAMPS
Akron 1920 Professionals

The Pros from Akron, Ohio, won the first championship of the new league.

NFL Grows

On June 24, 1922, the APFA changed its name to the National Football League (NFL), marking the official beginning of one of the most successful sports franchises in the world. Of the 14 teams to play in the league's first season, two are still playing today: the Chicago (now Arizona) Cardinals, and the Decatur Staleys (now called the Chicago Bears). The league didn't have an actual playoff game until 1932, when the Bears defeated Portsmouth, Ohio. This led to the league being organized into eastern and western divisions, with the top teams from each one meeting annually to play for the championship.

The early NFL needed good publicity so Jim Thorpe, football's biggest star, was named league president for the first season. He was a famous athlete who had also won Olympic gold in track and field.

African American Players

Though there was never an official ban, 1933 marked the last season any black players were present in the NFL for 12 seasons. Their absence finally ended in 1946, when the NFL's Rams agreed to **integrate** black players. They signed Kenneth Washington in March of that year, when the team moved to Los Angeles from Cleveland.

NFL TODAY

For decades after its founding, the NFL continually faced competition from other leagues. One of the most popular of these smaller leagues was the All-America Football Conference (AAFC), which had its first season in 1946. However, despite having strong teams, the AAFC was not financially stable. It shut down in 1949, and the NFL absorbed three of its most popular teams. A turning point for the league came in 1958. That year's championship game, between the Baltimore Colts and the New York Giants, is often called the "greatest game ever played." Besides being a thrilling game, and the first championship to end in **sudden death overtime**, it was also the first nationally televised championship.

With an audience of around 45 million, the 1958 championship was the beginning of the sport's massive rise in popularity throughout the country.

Final Merger

A direct result of this new popularity was the emergence of a new league in 1960. Called the American Football League, it was the first league to challenge the NFL's **supremacy** since the AAFC had folded. Throughout the decade, the leagues competed for players

The NFL champion Green Bay Packers defeated the AFL champion Kansas City Chiefs in the first Super Bowl, which was played in 1967.

and audiences. This led to the two leagues agreeing to a merger in 1966, which was completed in 1970. The leagues also agreed to hold a championship game at the end of each season between their respective number-one teams. This contest would come to be known as the Super Bowl. Super Bowls I to IV were actually between two separate leagues. After the merger was completed, the NFL was structured into two conferences: the National Football Conference, or NFC, which included most of the pre-merger NFL teams, and the American Football Conference, or AFC, which was made up of all of the former AFL teams, as well as three pre-merger NFL teams.

CATCH THIS!

The Green Bay Packers of 1965-67 won three NFL championships in a row, but no team has ever pulled off the feat in the Super Bowl era.

SUPER BOWL GAMES

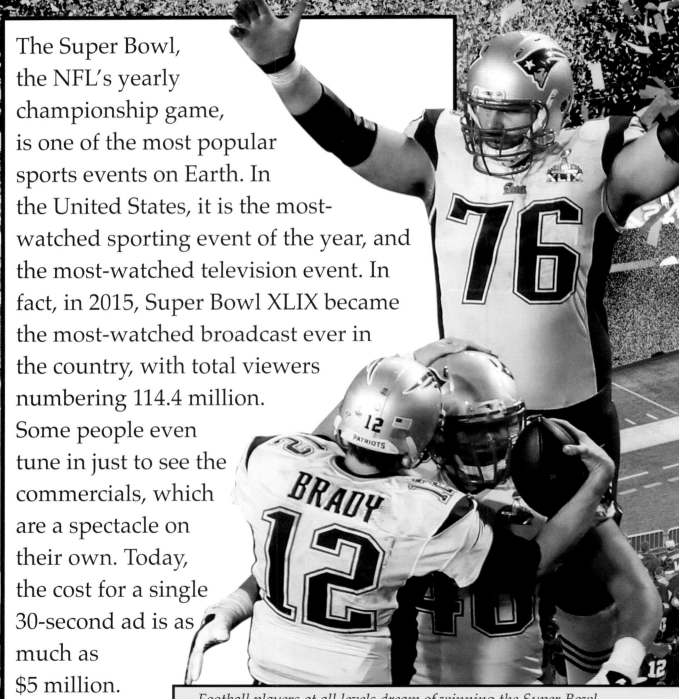

The Super Bowl, the NFL's yearly championship game, is one of the most popular sports events on Earth. In the United States, it is the most-watched sporting event of the year, and the most-watched television event. In fact, in 2015, Super Bowl XLIX became the most-watched broadcast ever in the country, with total viewers numbering 114.4 million. Some people even tune in just to see the commercials, which are a spectacle on their own. Today, the cost for a single 30-second ad is as much as $5 million.

Football players at all levels dream of winning the Super Bowl. The dream came true for the New England Patriots when they won their fourth Super Bowl XLIX in 2015.

Nationwide Party

Another popular aspect of the game is the halftime show, which often includes popular music stars. Like the ads, the halftime show often draws in viewers with no interest in the game itself. Many Americans think of the game as a national holiday, with many people organizing annual parties around it. The Super Bowl is also popular internationally. The only event with a larger annual audience is the Champions League final, Europe's top soccer championship.

Being invited to perform at halftime is a great honor for musicians. Katy Perry (left) and Lenny Kravitz starred at the Super Bowl in 2015.

It is also an honor for school bands to be invited to play at the Super Bowl.

Roman Numerals

Roman numerals have been used to number the Super Bowl since 1971. This is mostly done to avoid confusion, as the main season and the Super Bowl happen in different years. For example, the Super Bowl for the 2014 season took place on February 1, 2015. It would be confusing to call it Super Bowl 2014, because it took place in 2015, or to call it Super Bowl 2015, because it was for the 2014 season. Instead, it was called Super Bowl XLIX, marking the 49th game to be played in the championship's history.

Although gridiron football is most popular in North America, it also has fans around the world. The International Federation of American Football governs play in more than 70 countries. The IFAF World Championship of American Football is held every four years, similar to soccer's World Cup. Somewhat unsurprisingly, the United States currently holds the title.

When U.S. troops went abroad for World War II, they brought American football with them. Local residents would come out to watch their games, such as this one in Tsingtao, China, in 1943.

Today, teams all over Europe play American football in local and national leagues. The Austrian League is one of the most popular.

LEARNING MORE

There are many books you can read and websites you can visit to learn more about football.

Books

Sports Illustrated Kids Football: Then to WOW! by the Editors of Sports Illustrated Kids, 2014, Sports Illustrated

Legends: the Best Players, Games, and Teams in Football by Howard Bryant, 2015, Philomel Books

The Best of Everything Football Book by Shane Frederick, 2011, Capstone Press

Websites

Pro Football Hall-of-Fame
www.profootballhof.com

The Pro Football Hall-of-Fame has information about the history of football and the best football players of the past.

The Canadian Football Hall-of-Fame
www.cfhof.ca

The Canadian Football Hall-of-Fame has information about the history of CFL football, as well as information on teams and players.

GLOSSARY

down One of the four chances that an American football team has to move forward when it is their turn to have the ball

early adopter Someone who starts using a new idea, technology, or product as soon as it is available

elite The part of a group that has the highest quality or importance

evolved Changed over time

incorporated Added one thing into another

innovations New or improved ideas, devices, or products

integrate To unite into a whole; to bring different together parts of society, such as races

intervene To come between in order to stop or settle a dispute

mass-momentum The combined force of a group of people or objects moving together

offensive Team that is in possession of the ball

phenomenon A remarkable development

postseason Series of games which take place after the conclusion of the regular season

retractable Able to be pulled back

rival One of two or more trying to get what only one can have; a traditional opponent

snap-back Action in which the ball is thrown or handed backwards by the center to a recipient

sudden death overtime Extra playing time to break a tie, with the first team to score winning automatically

supremacy The state of being higher in rank or power than another

turning point An event marking an important change

unique One of a kind

voluntary According to free will, not forced

INDEX

All-America Football Conference (AAFC) 24

American Football Conference (AFC) 14, 17, 18, 25

American Football League 25

American Professional Football Association 22

American Professional Football Conference 22

AP poll 18

Army-Navy game 13

BCS National Championship 18, 19

Brallier, John 20

Camp, Walter 8, 9

Canadian Football League (CFL) 28, 29

Cochems, Eddie 15

College Football Hall-of-Fame 8

College Football Playoff 19

Division I 17

forward pass 7, 12, 15

Grey Cup 29

gridiron 5

Harvard University 7, 13, 28

Heffelfinger, William "Pudge" 20

helmets 13

Intercollegiate Athletic Association of the United States (IAAUS) 14

International Federation of American Football 30

MacCracken, Henry 14

McGill University 7, 28

Morgan Athletic Club 21

National Collegiate Athletic Association (NCCA) 3, 12, 14, 15, 17, 18, 19

National Football Conference (NFC) 25

National Football League (NFL) 3, 21, 22, 23, 24, 25, 26

Orange Bowl 16

Princeton 6, 13, 18

Reeves, Joseph 13

Robinson, Bradbury 15

Roosevelt, Theodore 13, 14

Rose Bowl 11, 16, 18

rugby 4, 5, 7, 8, 9, 28, 29

Rutgers 6

Snow, Neil 11

soccer 4, 5, 7, 8, 9, 27, 30

Super Bowl 3, 25, 26, 27

Thorpe, Jim 23

Washington, Kenneth 23

Welter, Jennifer 21

Yale 6, 8, 9, 13